Homemade Cookies

Author	Barbara Grunes and the Editorial Staff of Ideals Publishing Corporation
Director of Publishing	Patricia Pingry
Managing Editor	Marybeth Owens
Cookbook Editor	Julie Hogan
Manuscript Editor	Naomi Galbreath
Photographer	Gerald Koser
Food Styling	Liz Knuth
Editorial Assistants	Marjorie Friess, Linda Robinson
Typography	Kim Kaczanowski

IDEALS PUBLISHING CORP./11315 WATERTOWN PLANK ROAD/MILWAUKEE, WIS. 53226

Contents

Our sincere thanks to the following for their cooperation and help in supplying selected recipes from their test kitchens and files: American Butter Institute; California Table Grape Commission; National Cherry Growers & Industries Foundation; Oregon, Washington, California Pear Bureaus / Pacific Bartlett Growers, Inc.; Pacific Kitchens, Seattle, Washington; United Fresh Fruit & Vegetable Association; Washington State Apple Commission.

Cover recipes:
Upper left (from top): Apricot Sesame Thumbprints, 45
Upper right: Quick Chip Cookies, 44
Lower Right (from top): Drop Sugar Cookies (variation), 12; Fruit Swirls, 11; Pecan Butter Balls, 24
Lower left (from top): Hermits, 9; Pinwheels, 34; Chocolate Filled Sables, 32; Gingerbread Cookies, 45;
Drop Sugar Cookies (variations with colored sprinkles, jimmies, and walnuts), 12;
New England Macaroons, 37

ISBN 0-8249-3031-2
Copyright © MCMLXXXIV by Ideals Publishing Corp.
All rights reserved.
Printed and bound in the United States of America.

Published by Ideals Publishing Corporation
11315 Watertown Plank Road
Milwaukee, Wisconsin 53226
Published simultaneously in Canada

Cookie Hints

For best results with many of these recipes, first read the recipe through and observe the following:

- Organize your work area by assembling all of the necessary ingredients and utensils before beginning.
- Use standard measuring spoons and cups for accurate measuring. Level ingredients with a straight-edged spatula or knife.
- Prepare the baking sheet or pan before beginning to make the cookie dough. Grease the pan only if specified.
- Preheat the oven to the required temperature for 10 minutes.
- Place the baking sheet on the middle rack of the oven and bake only one sheet at a time.
- Unless otherwise indicated, remove the cookies from the baking sheet immediately after baking and cool on a wire rack.

Ingredients

Use only fresh, high-quality ingredients for best results.

Flour Most recipes call for all-purpose flour. Flour does not need to be sifted unless otherwise specified.

Eggs Use large eggs. For best results eggs should be kept at room temperature. When using egg whites, warm them slightly for optimum volume and be certain that the mixing bowl and beaters are free of grease.

Sugar In recipes calling for brown sugar, either light or dark brown can be used unless otherwise specified. To measure brown sugar accurately, pack it firmly into the measuring cup.

Butter In most recipes calling for butter, a good margarine can be substituted. Do not use shortening as a substitute for butter.

Cookie Check List

If your cookies do not turn out the way you hoped they would, check the following list for possible causes.

Cookies did not spread
✓ dough overmixed
✓ oven temperature too high

Cookies spread too much
✓ oven temperature too low
✓ baking sheet too heavily greased

Cookies stick to baking sheet
✓ baking sheet not cleaned between uses
✓ baking sheet not greased
✓ cookies underbaked
✓ cookies left too long on baking sheet before removal

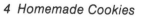

Drop Cookies

Fruit Drop Cookies

Makes 5½ dozen

1¼ cups all-purpose flour
¼ teaspoon baking soda
1 teaspoon cinnamon
½ teaspoon cloves
¼ teaspoon salt
½ cup butter *or* margarine, softened
1 cup packed light brown sugar
2 eggs
½ cup buttermilk
1 cup raisins
1 cup currants
¼ cup diced candied pineapple
½ cup diced candied citron
½ cup chopped walnuts

Combine flour, baking soda, cinnamon, cloves, and salt; set aside. In a large mixing bowl, cream butter and brown sugar until smooth. Add eggs, 1 at a time, beating well after each addition. Add dry ingredients alternately with buttermilk to creamed mixture, beating well after each addition. Stir in fruit and nuts. Drop batter by teaspoonfuls about 2 inches apart onto a greased baking sheet. Bake at 350° F. for 12 to 15 minutes or until edges are lightly browned. Remove from baking sheet to a wire rack to cool.

Golden Apple Cookies

Makes about 3½ dozen

1 cup vegetable shortening
¾ cup granulated sugar
¾ cup packed brown sugar
3 eggs
1 tablespoon grated orange peel
2 cups all-purpose flour
2 teaspoons baking powder
1 teaspoon cinnamon
½ teaspoon cloves
½ teaspoon nutmeg
½ teaspoon salt
3 or 4 Golden Delicious apples
2 cups rolled oats
½ cup raisins
½ cup chopped nuts

In a large mixing bowl, cream shortening and sugars until smooth. Blend in eggs and orange peel. Combine flour, baking powder, spices, and salt. Gradually add dry ingredients to creamed mixture; blend well. Pare, core, and chop apples to equal 3 cups. Stir in apples, oats, raisins, and nuts. Drop batter by rounded tablespoonfuls 2 inches apart onto a greased baking sheet. Bake at 350° F. for 15 to 17 minutes or until lightly browned. Remove from baking sheet to a wire rack to cool.

Drop Cookies

Candy Cookies

Makes about 6 dozen

In a large mixing bowl, cream butter and brown sugar until smooth. Blend in egg and vanilla. Sift together flour, baking soda, baking powder, and salt. Gradually add dry ingredients to creamed mixture; blend well. Stir in oats, candy, and nuts. Drop batter by rounded teaspoonfuls onto an ungreased baking sheet. Bake at 350° F. for 12 to 14 minutes or until golden. Remove from baking sheet to a wire rack to cool.

1 cup butter, softened
1 cup firmly packed light brown sugar
1 egg
1 teaspoon vanilla
1½ cups all-purpose flour
½ teaspoon baking soda
½ teaspoon baking powder
½ teaspoon salt
1 cup quick-cooking rolled oats
1 cup candy-coated chocolate pieces
½ cup chopped nuts

Chocolate Acorns

Makes 5 dozen

In a large mixing bowl, beat egg whites until soft peaks form. Add vinegar and salt; beat until stiff but not dry. Gradually add sugar, beating until stiff peaks form. Fold in vanilla, almonds, and melted unsweetened chocolate. Drop batter by rounded teaspoonfuls 1 inch apart onto a greased baking sheet. Bake at 250° for 25 to 30 minutes or until set. Remove from baking sheet to a wire rack to cool. Dip half of each cookie into the melted chocolate chips; sprinkle with pistachios.

3 egg whites
1 tablespoon vinegar
¼ teaspoon salt
1 cup sugar
1 teaspoon vanilla
½ pound ground blanched almonds
4 squares (1 ounce each), unsweetened baking chocolate, melted
1 cup semisweet chocolate chips, melted
½ cup finely chopped pistachio nuts

Currant Cakes

Makes 3 dozen

In a large mixing bowl, cream butter, lemon peel, and lemon juice until light. Add sugar; cream until light and fluffy. Add eggs; blend well. Mix flour and salt; gradually add to creamed mixture, beating until well blended. Stir in currants. Drop batter by teaspoonfuls onto a greased and floured baking sheet. Bake at 350° F. for 10 minutes or until set. Remove from baking sheet to a wire rack to cool.

1 cup butter, softened
1 teaspoon grated lemon peel
1 tablespoon lemon juice
1 cup sugar
3 eggs, well beaten
1¾ cups all-purpose flour
¼ teaspoon salt
¾ cup dried currants

Anise Drops

Makes 4 dozen

Combine flour and baking powder; set aside. In a large mixing bowl, beat eggs, sugar, and anise extract until light-colored. Stir in dry ingredients. Drop batter by teaspoonfuls about 2 inches apart onto a greased and floured baking sheet. Let stand at room temperature for 6 hours. Bake at 350° F. for 6 minutes. Remove from baking sheet to a wire rack to cool.

1½ **cups all-purpose flour**
¼ **teaspoon baking powder**
2 **eggs**
1 **cup sugar**
¼ **teaspoon anise extract**

Applesauce Cookies

Makes 5 dozen

Combine flour, baking powder, baking soda, salt, and spices; set aside. In a large mixing bowl, cream butter and sugar until smooth. Blend in egg. Add dry ingredients alternately with applesauce to creamed mixture, beating after each addition. Stir in raisins and cereal. Drop batter by teaspoonfuls about 2 inches apart onto a greased and floured baking sheet. Bake at 375° F. for 10 minutes or until golden. Remove from baking sheet to a wire rack to cool.

1¾ **cups all-purpose flour**
½ **teaspoon baking powder**
1 **teaspoon baking soda**
¼ **teaspoon salt**
1 **teaspoon cinnamon**
½ **teaspoon cloves**
½ **teaspoon nutmeg**
¾ **cup butter** *or* **margarine, softened**
1 **cup sugar**
1 **egg**
1 **cup thick sweetened applesauce**
½ **cup raisins**
1 **cup cornflakes, crushed**

Bear Paw Cookies

Makes about 3 dozen

In a large mixing bowl, cream butter and sugar until light and fluffy. Blend in chocolate syrup. Add eggs, 1 at a time, beating well after each addition. Blend in vanilla. Combine flour, baking powder, and salt. Add dry ingredients alternately with milk to chocolate mixture, beating well after each addition. Cover and chill 1 hour. Drop batter by heaping teaspoonfuls onto a greased baking sheet. Press 4 peanut halves into each cookie. Bake at 375° F. for 10 to 12 minutes or until centers spring back when lightly touched. Cool on the baking sheet 2 minutes; transfer to a wire rack to cool completely.

1 **cup butter** *or* **margarine, softened**
⅔ **cup sugar**
½ **cup chocolate-flavored syrup**
2 **eggs**
1 **teaspoon vanilla**
2⅓ **cups all-purpose flour**
2 **teaspoons baking powder**
1 **teaspoon salt**
¼ **cup milk**
Peanut halves or cashews

Hermits

Makes about 4½ dozen

¾ cup butter *or* margarine, softened
1½ cups packed dark brown sugar
2 eggs
2½ cups all-purpose flour
1 teaspoon baking soda
1 teaspoon cinnamon
¼ teaspoon salt
¼ teaspoon allspice
¼ teaspoon cloves
¾ cup raisins
¾ cup chopped nuts

In a large mixing bowl, cream butter and brown sugar until smooth. Add eggs; blend well. Combine flour, baking soda, cinnamon, salt, allspice, and cloves. Gradually blend dry ingredients into creamed mixture. Stir in raisins and nuts. Drop batter by rounded teaspoonfuls 2 inches apart onto a greased baking sheet. Bake at 375° F. for 8 to 10 minutes or until golden brown. Remove from baking sheet to a wire rack to cool.

Cranberry Charms

Makes about 6 dozen

2 cups fresh cranberries, coarsely chopped
1 cup granulated sugar, divided
1 cup vegetable shortening
1¼ cups packed light brown sugar
2 eggs
1¾ cups all-purpose flour
1 teaspoon salt
1 teaspoon baking powder
1 teaspoon baking soda
1 teaspoon cinnamon
1 teaspoon nutmeg
½ cup buttermilk or sour milk*
1 teaspoon vanilla
1 tablespoon grated orange peel
3 cups rolled oats
1 cup chopped nuts

In a small bowl, combine cranberries and ¾ cup granulated sugar; set aside for 30 minutes. In a large mixing bowl, cream remaining ¼ cup granulated sugar, shortening, brown sugar, and eggs until blended. Stir together flour, salt, baking powder, baking soda, and spices. Add dry ingredients alternately with buttermilk and vanilla to creamed mixture, beating well after each addition. Stir in orange peel, oats, nuts, and 1 cup of the cranberry-sugar mixture. Drop batter by tablespoonfuls 2 inches apart onto a greased baking sheet. Top cookies with remaining chopped cranberries. Bake at 400° F. for 10 minutes or until cookies are brown around the edges.

*To sour milk, mix 1½ teaspoons lemon juice into milk to equal ½ cup.

Fruit Swirls

Makes about 3 dozen

¾ **cup vegetable shortening**
¾ **cup granulated sugar**
¾ **cup packed brown sugar**
1 **egg**
1 **teaspoon vanilla**
2 **cups flour**
1½ **teaspoons baking powder**
¾ **teaspoon salt**
½ **cup raspberry preserves**

In a large mixing bowl, cream shortening and sugars until smooth. Add egg and vanilla; blend well. Stir together flour, baking powder, and salt. Gradually add to creamed mixture; blend until smooth. Stir in raspberry preserves until just blended. Do not overblend. Drop batter by teaspoonfuls about 2 inches apart onto an ungreased baking sheet. Bake at 375° F. for 12 to 15 minutes or until lightly browned. Remove from baking sheet to a wire rack to cool.

Rum Glazed Butterscotch Cookies

Makes 5 dozen

¾ **cup butter** *or* **margarine,**
  softened
½ **cup powdered sugar**
¼ **teaspoon salt**
1¾ **cups all-purpose flour**
1 **package (12 ounces)**
  butterscotch chips
¾ **cup chopped pecans**
  Rum Glaze

In a large mixing bowl, cream butter, powdered sugar, and salt until light and fluffy. Gradually add flour, beating until well blended. Stir in butterscotch chips and pecans. Drop dough by teaspoonfuls 1 inch apart onto a greased cookie sheet. Bake at 325° F. for 15 minutes or until cookies are firm but not brown. Remove from baking sheet to a wire rack to cool. Drizzle Rum Glaze evenly over each cookie. Let stand until glaze is firm.

Rum Glaze

2 **cups sifted powdered sugar**
¼ **cup light rum**

Combine powdered sugar and rum in a small mixing bowl; beat until smooth.

Vermont Drop Cookies

Makes 8 dozen

¾ **cup maple syrup**
¾ **cup packed dark brown sugar**
4 **eggs**
¾ **cup vegetable oil**
1 **teaspoon vanilla**
1 **cup skim milk powder**
2¾ **cups quick-cooking**
  rolled oats
1 **cup wheat germ**
1 **cup golden raisins**

In a large mixing bowl, combine maple syrup, brown sugar, eggs, oil, and vanilla; blend well. Stir in remaining ingredients in order given. Drop batter by teaspoonfuls onto a greased baking sheet. Bake at 350° F. for 12 to 15 minutes or until set. Remove from baking sheet to a wire rack to cool. Store in refrigerator.

Dark Chocolate Drop Cookies

Makes 4½ dozen

In a large mixing bowl, cream butter and brown sugar until smooth. Blend in egg, vanilla, and cooled chocolate. Stir together flour, baking soda, and salt. Add dry ingredients alternately with sour cream to chocolate mixture, beating well after each addition. Stir in pecans. Drop batter by teaspoonfuls 2 inches apart onto a greased and floured baking sheet. Bake at 350° F. for 10 minutes or until set. Remove from baking sheet to a wire rack to cool. Frost with Mocha Frosting.

- ½ cup butter *or* margarine, softened
- 1 cup packed brown sugar
- 1 egg
- 1 teaspoon vanilla
- 2 squares (1 ounce each) unsweetened baking chocolate, melted and cooled
- 2 cups all-purpose flour
- ½ teaspoon baking soda
- ¼ teaspoon salt
- ¾ cup dairy sour cream
- ½ cup chopped pecans
  Mocha Frosting

Mocha Frosting

In a medium mixing bowl, cream butter, cocoa, instant coffee, and salt until smooth. Gradually add powdered sugar, milk, and vanilla. Beat until frosting is smooth and of spreading consistency.

- ¼ cup butter, softened
- 2 tablespoons unsweetened cocoa
- 2 teaspoons instant coffee granules
- ¼ teaspoon salt
- 3 cups powdered sugar
- 3 tablespoons milk
- 1½ teaspoons vanilla

Drop Sugar Cookies

Makes about 5 dozen

In a large mixing bowl, cream shortening and sugar until smooth. Add eggs and vanilla; blend well. Stir together flour, baking soda, salt, and baking powder. Add dry ingredients alternately with sour cream to creamed mixture, beating well after each addition. Drop batter by teaspoonfuls 2 inches apart onto an ungreased baking sheet. Bake at 375° F. for 12 minutes or until just golden. Remove from baking sheet to a wire rack to cool.

- ⅔ cup vegetable shortening
- 1⅔ cups sugar
- 2 eggs
- 2 teaspoons vanilla
- 3½ cups sifted all-purpose flour
- ½ teaspoon baking soda
- 1 teaspoon salt
- 2 teaspoons baking powder
- ½ cup dairy sour cream

Bar Cookies

Fruit Bars

Makes 24 bars

½ cup butter, softened
1 cup sugar
2 eggs
1 teaspoon vanilla
¾ cup all-purpose flour
1 teaspoon baking powder
¼ teaspoon salt
1 cup chopped walnuts
½ cup red candied cherries,
   halved
1 cup sliced pitted dates
½ cup sliced soft dried apricots
½ cup sliced soft dried figs
   Chocolate Glaze

In a large mixing bowl, cream butter and sugar until smooth. Add eggs, 1 at a time, beating well after each addition. Blend in vanilla. Stir together flour, baking powder, and salt. Gradually add dry ingredients to creamed mixture; blend well. Stir in nuts and fruit. Spread batter in a greased 9-inch square baking pan. Bake at 350° F. for 45 minutes. Cool in pan before cutting into bars. Spread with Chocolate Glaze. Store in an airtight container.

Chocolate Glaze

⅓ cup sugar
3 tablespoons water
1 cup semisweet chocolate
   chips
3 tablespoons marshmallow
   creme
1 to 2 tablespoons hot water

In a small saucepan, combine sugar and 3 tablespoons water. Bring to a boil; remove from heat. Stir in chocolate chips until melted. Blend in marshmallow creme. Add hot water, 1 teaspoonful at a time, stirring until desired consistency is reached.

Irish Mist Bars

Makes 18 bars

½ cup butter, softened
1½ cups packed light brown
   sugar, divided
1 cup all-purpose flour
1 tablespoon all-purpose flour
¼ teaspoon salt
2 eggs
1 tablespoon Irish Mist liqueur
1 cup chopped nuts

In a large mixing bowl, combine butter, ½ cup brown sugar, and 1 cup flour; blend until crumbly. Firmly press crumb mixture into a 9-inch square baking pan. Bake at 350° F. for 10 minutes; set aside to cool. In a large mixing bowl, combine remaining 1 cup brown sugar, 1 tablespoon flour, and salt; blend well. Add eggs, 1 at a time, beating well after each addition. Blend in liqueur; stir in nuts. Spread batter evenly over cooled crust. Bake at 350° F. for 20 minutes. Cool in pan before cutting into bars.

Peanut Brittle Bars

Makes 36 bars

1 cup all-purpose flour
¼ teaspoon baking soda
½ teaspoon cinnamon
½ cup butter, softened
½ cup packed light brown sugar
1 teaspoon vanilla
1 egg, beaten
1 cup finely chopped salted
  peanuts, divided

Sift together flour, baking soda, and cinnamon; set aside. In a large mixing bowl, cream butter and brown sugar until smooth. Blend in vanilla and 2 tablespoons of the egg; reserve remaining egg. Gradually add dry ingredients, blending well. Stir in ½ cup peanuts. Spread batter in a greased 14 x 10-inch baking pan. Brush with reserved egg. Sprinkle with remaining ½ cup peanuts. Bake at 325° F. for 20 minutes. Cool in pan 5 minutes before cutting into bars.

Jeweled Coconut Chews

Makes 16 bars

⅓ cup butter *or* margarine,
  softened
⅓ cup powdered sugar
¾ cup all-purpose flour
1 cup seedless green grapes
½ cup packed brown sugar
¼ cup chopped walnuts
¼ cup flaked coconut
1 tablespoon flour
1 egg
¼ teaspoon baking powder
¼ teaspoon salt
¼ teaspoon almond extract
⅛ teaspoon nutmeg

In a small mixing bowl, cream butter and powdered sugar until smooth. Add ¾ cup flour; mix until crumbly. Press crumb mixture into an ungreased 8-inch square baking pan. Bake at 350° F. for 15 minutes or until light brown. In a large bowl, combine remaining ingredients; blend well. Spread over baked crust. Bake at 350° F. for 25 minutes or until golden brown. Cool in pan before cutting into bars.

Raspberry Bars

Makes 24 bars

¾ cup margarine, softened
1 cup packed light brown sugar
1¾ cups all-purpose flour
½ teaspoon baking soda
½ teaspoon salt
1½ cups rolled oats
1 jar (18 ounces) raspberry jam

In a large mixing bowl, cream margarine and brown sugar until smooth. Stir together flour, baking soda, and salt. Gradually add dry ingredients to creamed mixture; mix until crumbly. Stir in oats. Press half of the crumb mixture into a greased 13 x 9-inch baking pan. Spread with raspberry jam. Sprinkle remaining crumb mixture over the top; press lightly into jam. Bake at 400° F. for 20 minutes or until lightly browned. Cool 5 minutes before cutting into bars.

Raspberry Bars, this page

Chocolate Bars

Makes 36 bars

In a large mixing bowl, combine butter, flour, and salt; mix until crumbly. Press crumb mixture into a greased and floured 9-inch square baking pan. Bake at 350° F. for 15 minutes. In a small mixing bowl, beat eggs and sugar until smooth. Stir in 1 cup nuts, vanilla, salt, and 2 tablespoons flour; blend well. Spread nut mixture over baked crust. Bake at 350° F. for 15 minutes; set aside to cool. In the top of a double boiler, melt chocolate chips over hot but not boiling water. Blend in corn syrup and water. Spread chocolate mixture evenly over cooled layer. Sprinkle with chopped nuts. Let stand overnight. Cut into bars.

¼ cup butter *or* margarine, softened
1 cup sifted all-purpose flour
¼ teaspoon salt
2 eggs, lightly beaten
¾ cup packed light brown sugar
1 cup chopped walnuts
1 teaspoon vanilla
¼ teaspoon salt
2 tablespoons all-purpose flour
1 package (6 ounces) semisweet chocolate chips
¼ cup light corn syrup
1 tablespoon water
Chopped walnuts

Chocolate Chip Butterscotch Bars

Makes 24 bars

Stir together flour, baking powder, and salt; set aside. In a medium saucepan, melt butter. Add brown sugar; stir over low heat until sugar melts. Transfer to a large mixing bowl. Add eggs, 1 at a time, beating well after each addition. Blend in vanilla. Add dry ingredients; blend well. Stir in 2 cups chocolate chips and nuts. Spread batter in a greased 8-inch square baking pan. Bake at 350° F. for 30 minutes. Cool in pan. Frost with Butterscotch Frosting. Sprinkle with remaining ½ cup chocolate chips. Cut into bars.

¾ cup all-purpose flour
½ teaspoon baking powder
½ teaspoon salt
½ cup butter *or* margarine
1 cup packed dark brown sugar
2 eggs
1 teaspoon vanilla
2½ cups semisweet chocolate chips, divided
½ cup chopped walnuts
Butterscotch Frosting

Butterscotch Frosting

In a small mixing bowl, cream butter and sugar until smooth. Blend in cream and vanilla. If frosting is too soft to spread, chill 10 minutes before using.

¼ cup butter *or* margarine, softened
½ cup packed dark brown sugar
1 tablespoon half-and-half
¼ teaspoon vanilla

English Toffee Bars
Makes about 6 dozen

1 cup butter, softened
1 cup sugar
1 egg yolk
1¾ cups all-purpose flour
1 teaspoon cinnamon
1 egg white, lightly beaten
1 cup chopped pecans
3 tablespoons milk
1 teaspoon instant coffee
   granules
2 squares (1 ounce each)
   semisweet chocolate

In a large mixing bowl, cream butter and sugar until smooth. Add egg yolk; blend well. Sift together flour and cinnamon. Gradually work dry ingredients into creamed mixture until crumbly. Press crumb mixture evenly into a buttered 15 x 10-inch baking pan. Brush top with egg white. Sprinkle with pecans; press lightly into dough. Bake at 275° F. for 1 hour. While the crust is baking, heat milk, coffee granules, and chocolate in a saucepan over low heat, stirring until chocolate melts. Cut into 1½-inch bars. Drizzle with melted chocolate mixture. Cool in pan on a wire rack.

Pear and Graham Cracker Bars
Makes about 30 bars

2 ripe Bartlett pears
   Whole graham crackers
1 cup packed light brown sugar
½ cup butter *or* margarine
¼ cup milk
1 cup flaked coconut
1 cup graham cracker crumbs
1 package (6 ounces)
   butterscotch chips

Core and dice pears to measure 1½ cups. Line a 13 x 9-inch baking pan with whole graham crackers. In a medium saucepan, combine diced pears, brown sugar, butter, milk, coconut, and graham cracker crumbs; bring to a boil. Boil until thick, stirring constantly. Spread pear mixture over crackers. Top with layer of whole crackers. In the top of a double boiler, melt butterscotch chips. Spread melted chips over crackers. Cut between crackers into bars. Store in the refrigerator.

Orange Bars
Makes 36 bars

½ cup butter, softened
1½ cups all-purpose flour
¼ cup sugar
3 tablespoons grated orange
   peel
1 egg
1 package (6 ounces)
   semisweet chocolate chips

In a large mixing bowl, cut butter into flour until crumbly. Blend in sugar, orange peel, and egg. Roll out dough on a lightly floured surface to a ¼-inch thickness. Cut into 2 x 1-inch bars. Place bars about 1 inch apart on a lightly greased baking sheet. Bake at 400° F. for 8 to 10 minutes or until lightly browned. Remove from baking sheet to a wire rack to cool. Melt chocolate in the top of a double boiler over hot but not boiling water. Dip each bar halfway into the melted chocolate. Place on a sheet of waxed paper until the chocolate sets, about 10 minutes.

Double Chocolate Crumble Bars

Makes about 4 dozen

In a large mixing bowl, cream butter and sugar until smooth. Blend in eggs and vanilla. Stir together flour, pecans, cocoa, baking powder, and salt. Gradually add dry ingredients to the creamed mixture; blend well. Spread batter in a greased 13 x 9-inch baking pan. Bake at 350° F. for 15 to 20 minutes or until light brown. Sprinkle marshmallows evenly over top. Bake for 3 minutes. Cool in pan on a wire rack. In a small saucepan, melt chocolate chips and peanut butter over low heat, stirring constantly. Stir in cereal. Spread on top of cooled crust. Refrigerate until firm. Cut into bars. Store in the refrigerator.

- ½ cup butter, softened
- ¾ cup sugar
- 2 eggs
- 1 teaspoon vanilla
- ¾ cup all-purpose flour
- ½ cup chopped pecans
- 2 tablespoons unsweetened cocoa
- ¼ teaspoon baking powder
- ¼ teaspoon salt
- 2 cups miniature marshmallows
- 1 package (6 ounces) semisweet chocolate chips
- 1 cup peanut butter
- 1½ cups crispy rice cereal

Filbert Chocolate Cream Bars

Makes 6 dozen bars

Spread nuts in a shallow baking pan. Toast in oven for 5 to 10 minutes, stirring occasionally. In a medium saucepan, combine butter, sugar, cocoa, vanilla, salt, and egg. Cook over low heat, stirring constantly until mixture thickens and becomes glossy. Combine cookie crumbs, nuts, and coconut. Add cocoa mixture; blend well. Press firmly into a 9-inch square baking pan. Spread Mint Frosting on top. Chill until frosting is firm. In the top of a double boiler, melt chocolate over hot but not boiling water. Spread chocolate over frosting. Let stand until chocolate is partially set. Cut into bars. Refrigerate until ready to serve.

- 1 cup chopped filberts *or* almonds
- ½ cup butter
- ¼ cup sugar
- 2 tablespoons unsweetened cocoa
- 2 teaspoons vanilla
- ¼ teaspoon salt
- 1 egg, beaten
- 1¾ cups vanilla wafer crumbs (about 45 wafers)
- ½ cup flaked coconut
  Mint Frosting
- 4 squares (1 ounce each) semisweet baking chocolate

Mint Frosting

In a small mixing bowl, cream butter and egg until smooth. Blend in peppermint extract. Gradually add powdered sugar, beating until smooth and creamy.

- ¼ cup butter, softened
- 1 egg
- ½ teaspoon peppermint extract
- 2 cups sifted powdered sugar

Brownies

Light Nut Brownies

Makes 3 dozen

In a large mixing bowl, cream butter. Gradually add 1 cup flour and salt; blend well. Spread the batter in a greased and floured 9-inch square baking pan. Bake at 350° F. for 15 minutes; cool. In a small bowl, beat eggs and sugar until light. Stir in ¾ cup nuts, vanilla, and 2 tablespoons flour. Spoon over cooled crust. Return to oven. Bake at 350° F. for 15 minutes. Cool in pan. Spread with Chocolate Frosting. Sprinkle with remaining ¼ cup nuts. Cut into squares.

¼ cup butter *or* margarine, softened
1 cup all-purpose flour
¼ teaspoon salt
2 eggs
¾ cup packed light brown sugar
1 cup chopped walnuts, divided
1 teaspoon vanilla
2 tablespoons all-purpose flour
Chocolate Frosting

Chocolate Frosting

In the top of a double boiler, melt chocolate chips over hot but not boiling water. Blend in corn syrup and water.

1 cup semisweet chocolate chips
¼ cup light corn syrup
1 tablespoon water

Blonde Brownies

Makes 1½ dozen

In a large mixing bowl, cream butter and sugar until smooth. Add egg yolk, whole egg, and vanilla; blend well. Sift together flour, baking powder, and salt. Gradually add to creamed mixture, beating until well blended. Pour batter into a greased 9-inch square baking pan. Stir together brown sugar, nuts, and egg white. Spread over the batter. Bake at 325° F. for 1 hour or until brownie begins to pull away from sides of the pan. Cool in pan before cutting into squares.

½ cup butter, softened
1 cup sugar
1 egg yolk
1 whole egg
1 teaspoon vanilla
2 cups all-purpose flour
1 teaspoon baking powder
½ teaspoon salt
1 cup packed brown sugar
1 cup chopped walnuts
1 egg white

Moist Chocolate Brownies

Makes 1½ dozen

1 box (8 ounces) semisweet
  chocolate
7 tablespoons butter
2 eggs
¾ cup sugar
1 teaspoon vanilla
¼ cup all-purpose flour
1 cup coarsely chopped
  walnuts

In the top of a double boiler, melt chocolate and butter over warm water. Remove from heat. In a large mixing bowl, beat eggs and sugar until light and fluffy. Blend in chocolate mixture and vanilla. Stir in flour and nuts. Pour batter into a greased 8-inch square baking pan. Bake at 375° F. for 30 minutes or until brownie begins to pull away from sides of the pan. Cool in pan before cutting into squares.

Toffee Crunch Brownies

Makes 2 dozen

4 squares (1 ounce each)
  unsweetened baking
  chocolate
½ cup butter
4 eggs
1 cup sugar
2 teaspoons vanilla
¾ cup all-purpose flour
¼ teaspoon salt
6 ounces toffee candy bars,
  chopped

In the top of a double boiler, melt chocolate and butter over warm water. Remove from heat. In a large mixing bowl, beat eggs and sugar until light and fluffy; blend into chocolate mixture. Blend in vanilla, flour, and salt. Stir in toffee candy. Spoon mixture into a greased 9-inch square baking pan. Bake at 325° F. for 45 minutes. Cool in pan before cutting into squares.

Two-Toned Brownies

Makes 16

¼ cup butter *or margarine,*
  softened
¼ cup sugar
¼ cup light corn syrup
1 egg
1 cup all-purpose flour
½ teaspoon baking powder
¼ teaspoon salt
2 squares (1 ounce each)
  semisweet chocolate, melted
1 package (3 ounces) cream
  cheese, softened

In a large mixing bowl, cream butter and sugar until smooth. Blend in corn syrup and egg. Combine flour, baking powder, and salt. Add dry ingredients to creamed mixture; blend well. To ½ cup of the batter blend in melted chocolate. To remaining batter, add cream cheese; beat until smooth. Spread cream cheese batter into a greased 9-inch square baking pan. Carefully spread chocolate batter on top. With a knife, swirl chocolate batter through cream cheese batter. Bake at 350° F. for 40 to 45 minutes or until brownie begins to pull away from sides of the pan. Cool in pan before cutting into squares.

Marshmallow Pecan Brownies

Makes 3 dozen

In a small saucepan, melt chocolate and butter over low heat, stirring constantly; set aside to cool. In a large mixing bowl, beat eggs lightly. Blend in sugar, vanilla, and melted chocolate mixture. Stir together flour, baking powder, and salt; gradually blend into chocolate mixture. Stir in pecans. Spread batter in a greased 11 x 7-inch baking pan. Bake at 325° F. for 25 minutes or until brownie begins to pull away from sides of the pan. Sprinkle marshmallows evenly over top. Return to oven for 3 to 4 minutes or until marshmallows are soft. Cool before spreading with Mocha Chocolate Frosting. Cut into 2 x 1-inch bars.

2 squares (1 ounce each) unsweetened baking chocolate
½ cup butter *or* **margarine**
2 eggs
1 cup sugar
1 teaspoon vanilla
1¼ cups sifted all-purpose flour
½ teaspoon baking powder
½ teaspoon salt
1 cup chopped pecans
2 cups miniature marshmallows
Mocha Chocolate Frosting

Mocha Chocolate Frosting

In a small saucepan, melt chocolate and butter over low heat, stirring constantly. Blend in coffee, vanilla, and salt. Gradually beat in powdered sugar, adding water, if necessary, to bring to spreading consistency.

1 square (1 ounce) unsweetened chocolate
2 tablespoons butter
1 teaspoon instant coffee granules
½ teaspoon vanilla
⅛ teaspoon salt
2 cups powdered sugar
2 to 3 tablespoons hot water

Batter-Up Brownies

Makes 2 dozen

In a small saucepan, melt the shortening; cool slightly. Stir together flour, baking powder, and salt. Add shortening, sugar, and eggs to flour mixture; blend well. Blend in peanut butter and vanilla. Stir in peanuts and chocolate chips. Spread batter in a greased 13 x 9-inch baking pan. Bake at 350° F. for 25 to 30 minutes or until brownie begins to pull away from sides of the pan. Cool in pan before cutting into squares.

½ cup vegetable shortening
1 cup all-purpose flour
½ teaspoon baking powder
½ teaspoon salt
1½ cups sugar
3 eggs
½ cup peanut butter
1 teaspoon vanilla
1 cup chopped peanuts
1 package (6 ounces) semisweet chocolate chips

Molded, Pressed, and Filled Cookies

Walnut Crescents

Makes about 5 dozen

In a large mixing bowl, cream butter and sugar until smooth. Add vanilla; blend well. Gradually blend in flour; stir in nuts. Shape spoonfuls of dough into rolls about 3 inches long. Place on an ungreased baking sheet. Pull ends down to form a crescent. Bake at 350° F. for 15 to 16 minutes or until golden. Cool slightly on pan. Remove to wire rack to cool completely. Dip ends in Chocolate Glaze, then in jimmies or coconut.

1 cup butter, softened
¾ cup sugar
1½ teaspoons vanilla
2½ cups all-purpose flour
1 cup finely chopped walnuts
Chocolate Glaze
Chocolate jimmies *or* flaked coconut

Chocolate Glaze

In a small saucepan, combine all ingredients. Cook over low heat, stirring constantly until smooth.

1½ ounces semisweet baking chocolate
1½ teaspoons light corn syrup
1½ teaspoons cream

Pecan Butter Balls

Makes about 3 dozen

In a large mixing bowl, cream butter and sugar until light and fluffy. Blend in vanilla. Gradually add flour; blend well. Stir in nuts. Cover and chill until firm. Shape dough into 1-inch balls. Place on a greased baking sheet. Bake at 350° F. for 20 minutes or until golden brown. Remove from baking sheet to a wire rack to cool.

1 cup butter, softened
½ cup powdered sugar
½ teaspoon vanilla
1¾ cups all-purpose flour
½ cup chopped pecans

Keep butter cookie dough covered while it is being refrigerated. This will prevent the delicate dough from absorbing food odors and drying out.

Pressed Peanut Butter Cookies

Makes about 2½ dozen

1 cup butter, softened
1 cup packed brown sugar
1 egg
1 cup creamy peanut butter
1 teaspoon vanilla
2 cups all-purpose flour
1 teaspoon baking soda
¼ teaspoon salt
Peanut Butter Filling
Granulated sugar

In a large bowl, cream butter and brown sugar until smooth. Add egg, peanut butter, and vanilla; blend well. Stir together flour, baking soda, and salt; gradually blend into peanut butter mixture. Cover and chill 30 minutes. Prepare Peanut Butter Filling. Fill cookie press. Using the bar attachment, press bars about 2 inches long onto a lightly greased baking sheet. Top each with ½ teaspoon filling. Press another bar directly onto filling. Press edges gently together. Sprinkle with granulated sugar. Bake at 350° F. for 10 minutes. Remove from baking sheet to a wire rack to cool.

Peanut Butter Filling

½ cup crunchy peanut butter
2 tablespoons butter, softened
¼ cup sugar

In a bowl, blend all ingredients.

Chocolate Mint Wafers

Makes about 5 dozen

⅔ cup butter, softened
1 cup sugar
1 egg
2 cups all-purpose flour
¾ cup unsweetened cocoa
½ teaspoon salt
1 teaspoon baking powder
¼ cup milk
Mint Filling

In a large mixing bowl, cream butter and sugar until smooth. Add egg; beat until light and fluffy. Stir together flour, cocoa, salt, and baking powder. Add dry ingredients alternately with milk to creamed mixture, beating well after each addition. Roll out dough on a floured surface to ⅛-inch thickness. Cut out with a 2-inch round cookie cutter. Place on a greased baking sheet. Bake at 350° F. for 8 minutes. Remove from baking sheet to a wire rack to cool. Spread half of the cookies with Mint Filling. Top with remaining cookies.

Mint Filling

½ cup sifted powdered sugar
2 drops peppermint extract
3 to 4 tablespoons milk

In a small bowl, blend all ingredients until filling is of spreading consistency.

Chocolate Pecan Tarts

Makes about 4 dozen

½ **cup butter** *or* **margarine,**
   softened
2 **packages (3 ounces each)**
   cream cheese, softened
½ **cup vegetable shortening**
2 **cups all-purpose flour**
   Chocolate Pecan Filling

In a large mixing bowl, cream butter, cream cheese, and shortening until smooth. Gradually add flour; blend well. Cover and chill until firm. Shape dough into 1-inch balls. Place balls in ungreased miniature muffin cups. Press firmly onto bottom and up sides of muffin cups; set aside. Prepare Chocolate Pecan Filling. Spoon a heaping teaspoonful of filling into each tart shell. Bake at 350° F. for 20 to 25 minutes or until tarts are golden brown. Cool in pan on a wire rack.

Chocolate Pecan Filling

2 **eggs**
¾ **cup sugar**
3 **tablespoons cornstarch**
½ **cup butter** *or* **margarine,**
   melted
1 **teaspoon vanilla**
2 **tablespoons light corn syrup**
¾ **cup miniature semisweet**
   chocolate chips
½ **cup finely chopped pecans**

In a small bowl, combine eggs, sugar, and cornstarch; blend well. Blend in butter, vanilla, and corn syrup. Stir in chocolate chips and pecans.

Cherry Thumbprints

Makes about 3½ dozen

1½ **cups all-purpose flour**
¼ **cup sugar**
½ **cup butter, softened**
1 **egg**
1 **teaspoon vanilla**
¼ **teaspoon salt**
¼ **cup finely chopped nuts**
1 **teaspoon grated lemon peel**
   Powdered sugar
   Cherry Filling

In a large mixing bowl, combine flour, sugar, butter, egg, vanilla, and salt; blend well. Stir in nuts and lemon peel. Gently shape dough into 1-inch balls. Place on an ungreased baking sheet. Press thumb deeply into center of each ball. Bake at 350° F. for 10 minutes or until cookies are set. Remove from baking sheet to a wire rack to cool. Roll cookies in powdered sugar. Prepare Cherry Filling. Spoon one cherry into the center of each cookie. For best results, fill cookies on the day they are to be served.

Cherry Filling

1 **can (16 or 17 ounces) pitted**
   dark sweet cherries, drained;
   reserve ⅓ **cup juice**
2 **teaspoons cornstarch**
   Dash salt

In a saucepan, combine reserved cherry juice and cornstarch. Add salt. Cook over medium heat, stirring constantly until thickened and clear. Stir in the cherries. Let stand until cool.

Chocolate Pecan Tarts, this page
Pink Party Sandwiches, 29

Molded, Pressed, and Filled Cookies

Cream Cheese Butter Crisps

Makes about 7 dozen

In a large mixing bowl, cream butter and cream cheese until smooth. Gradually blend in sugar. Add egg yolk and vanilla; blend well. Stir together flour, salt, and baking powder; gradually blend into creamed mixture. Fill cookie press with dough. Use desired attachment to form cookies on an ungreased baking sheet. Bake at 350° F. for 12 to 15 minutes or until golden. Remove from baking sheet to a wire rack to cool.

- 1 cup butter, softened
- 1 package (3 ounces) cream cheese, softened
- 1 cup sugar
- 1 egg yolk
- 1 teaspoon vanilla
- 2 cups all-purpose flour
- ½ teaspoon salt
- ¼ teaspoon baking powder

Spritz Cookies

Makes about 7 dozen

In a large mixing bowl, cream butter and sugar until light and fluffy. Blend in egg and almond extract. Gradually mix in flour. Add food coloring; blend well. Fill a cookie press with dough. Using star or bar attachment, form cookies on an ungreased baking sheet. Sprinkle with colored sugar. Bake at 350° F. for 8 to 10 minutes or until golden. Remove from baking sheet to a wire rack to cool.

- 1 cup butter, softened
- ½ cup sugar
- 1 egg
- ½ teaspoon almond extract
- 2¼ cups all-purpose flour
  Food coloring, optional
  Colored decorating sugar, optional

Filbert Lemon Logs

Makes about 4 dozen

In a large mixing bowl, cream butter and powdered sugar until smooth. Add egg, lemon peel, and juice; blend well. Stir together flour and salt. Gradually blend flour mixture into creamed mixture. Cover and chill until firm. Shape dough into 2 x ¾-inch rolls. Roll in nuts. Place on a greased baking sheet. Bake at 350° F. for 12 to 15 minutes or until set. Remove from baking sheet to a wire rack to cool.

- 1 cup butter, softened
- ¾ cup powdered sugar
- 1 egg
- 1½ tablespoons grated lemon peel
- 1 tablespoon lemon juice
- 2¼ cups all-purpose flour
- ¼ teaspoon salt
- ¾ cup finely chopped filberts

Butter can be taken directly from the refrigerator and creamed if each stick is cut into about eight pieces. Keep the mixer on low speed when starting to cream the butter, and increase speed as the butter softens.

Pink Party Sandwiches

Makes about 4 dozen

1¼ cups butter, softened
2 cups sugar
2 eggs
1 teaspoon vanilla
1½ cups sifted all-purpose flour
1½ cups cornstarch
½ teaspoon cream of tartar
Pink Butter Filling

In a large mixing bowl, cream butter and sugar until smooth. Blend in eggs and vanilla. Stir together flour, cornstarch, and cream of tartar. Gradually add flour mixture to creamed mixture; blend well. Chill dough until firm. Roll out dough on a lightly floured surface to ⅛-inch thickness. Cut out with a floured 3-inch cookie cutter. Place on a greased baking sheet. Bake at 400° F. for about 8 minutes or until edges are golden brown. Remove from baking sheet to a wire rack to cool. Fill cookies with Pink Butter Filling.

Pink Butter Filling

¼ cup butter, softened
2 cups sifted powdered sugar
¼ cup whipping cream
1 teaspoon vanilla
Red food coloring

Cream butter until light and fluffy. Gradually beat in sugar, cream, and vanilla. Tint with red food coloring. Beat until filling is of spreading consistency.

Filled Almond Cookies

Makes about 2 dozen

½ cup butter, softened
⅓ cup sugar
1 egg, separated
1¼ cups all-purpose flour
½ teaspoon salt
¼ cup ground almonds
½ cup sugar
Grape jelly

In a large mixing bowl, cream butter and sugar until smooth. Add egg yolk; beat until light and fluffy. Combine flour and salt. Gradually add flour mixture to creamed mixture; blend well. Roll out dough on a lightly floured surface to ⅛-inch thickness. Cut out half of the dough with a floured 2½-inch round cookie cutter. Cut out the remaining dough with a 2-inch scalloped cookie cutter; use a thimble to remove centers. Lightly beat egg white. Combine almonds and sugar on a sheet of waxed paper. Brush each scalloped cookie with egg and then dip in almond mixture. Place cookies, coated sides up, on a greased and floured baking sheet. Bake at 375° F. for 6 minutes. Cookies should not brown. Remove from baking sheet to a wire rack to cool. Spread round cookies with a little jelly. Place scalloped cookies on top of the round cookies. Fill centers with grape jelly.

Almond Butter Cookies

Makes about 5 dozen

1 cup butter, softened
3 tablespoons sugar
1 teaspoon almond extract
2 cups all-purpose flour
½ teaspoon salt
   Sliced, unblanched almonds
   Powdered Sugar Frosting

In a large mixing bowl, cream butter and sugar until light and fluffy. Blend in almond extract. Stir together flour and salt. Gradually add flour mixture to creamed mixture; blend well. Cover and chill until firm. Shape into ¾-inch balls. Place on an ungreased baking sheet. With the bottom of a glass dipped in flour, flatten balls to ¼-inch thickness. Bake at 400° F. for 5 to 6 minutes. Remove from baking sheet to a wire rack to cool. Spread about ½ teaspoon frosting on each cookie. Top with a sliced almond.

Powdered Sugar Frosting

1 cup sifted powdered sugar
1 tablespoon butter, softened
½ teaspoon vanilla
1½ tablespoons hot water
   Green food coloring

In a small bowl, combine sugar, butter, and vanilla; blend well. Add water; beat until of spreading consistency. Tint with green food coloring.

Crisp Chocolate Rolls

Makes about 3 dozen

½ cup butter, softened
½ cup sugar
1 teaspoon vanilla
2 egg whites
⅔ cup all-purpose flour
   Creamy Chocolate Filling

In a large mixing bowl, cream butter, sugar, and vanilla until light and fluffy. Add egg whites; blend well. Gradually add flour; blend well. Drop batter by teaspoonfuls 1 inch apart on an ungreased baking sheet. Spread with the back of a spoon into 3-inch rounds. Bake at 375° F. for 5 minutes or until edges are light brown. Working with 1 cookie at a time, loosen from baking sheet with a spatula and then quickly roll tightly around a pencil. Transfer to a wire rack to cool, seam side down. With a pastry bag, soda straw, or wooden pick fill rolls with Creamy Chocolate Filling.

Creamy Chocolate Filling

3 squares (1 ounce each) semisweet chocolate
¼ teaspoon vegetable oil, butter, *or* margarine

In a small saucepan, melt chocolate and oil over low heat, stirring constantly.

Rolled and Refrigerated Cookies

Dutch Butter Cookies

Makes about 4 dozen

In a large mixing bowl, cream butter and powdered sugar until smooth. Add egg and lemon peel; blend well. Stir together flour, baking powder, mace, and salt. Gradually add to creamed mixture; knead until smooth. Cover with plastic wrap and chill 2 hours. Roll out dough on a lightly floured surface to ⅛-inch thickness. Cut out with floured cookie cutters. Place on a lightly greased baking sheet. Bake at 350° F. for 15 minutes or until golden. Remove from baking sheet to a wire rack to cool. Frost, if desired.

½ cup butter, softened
1 cup powdered sugar
1 egg
1 tablespoon grated lemon peel
2½ cups sifted cake flour
½ teaspoon baking powder
¼ teaspoon mace
¼ teaspoon salt

Chocolate Filled Sables

Makes about 54 double cookies

Crumble almond paste into a large bowl. Add butter; blend with hands until smooth. Add sugar, eggs, and vanilla; beat until light and fluffy. Stir together flours and salt. Gradually add flour mixture to almond mixture; blend well. Cover and chill for 3 hours. Divide dough in half. Roll out one half between sheets of waxed paper to ⅛-inch thickness. Transfer dough and paper to a small baking sheet. Place in freezer for 10 minutes. Carefully peel off both sheets of waxed paper. Cut out dough with a floured 2-inch cookie cutter. Roll out remaining dough and chill as above. Cut dough into rounds. Remove centers with a thimble. Place cookies on a large baking sheet. Bake at 375° F. for 5 minutes or until golden. Remove from baking sheet to a wire rack to cool. Spread bottoms of whole cookies with Chocolate Frosting. Dust cut-out rounds with powdered sugar. Press onto whole cookies. Fill centers, if desired.

1 package (8 ounces) almond paste
1 cup butter or margarine, softened
1 cup sugar
2 eggs
¾ teaspoon vanilla
2 cups plus 2 tablespoons sifted flour
1⅜ cups sifted cake flour
¾ teaspoon salt
Chocolate Frosting (recipe on page 20)
Powdered sugar

Vanilla Sandwich Cookies

Makes about 3 dozen

¾ cup butter, softened
¼ cup packed light brown sugar
¼ cup sugar
1 egg yolk
1 teaspoon vanilla
1¾ cups all-purpose flour
Vanilla Frosting
Pecan halves

In a large mixing bowl, cream butter and sugars until smooth. Add egg yolk and vanilla; blend well. Gradually blend in flour. Chill until dough is firm. Divide dough in half. Shape each half into a 7 x 1½-inch roll. Wrap in plastic wrap and chill overnight. Cut into ⅛-inch slices; place about 1 inch apart on an ungreased baking sheet. Bake at 350° F. for 8 to 10 minutes. Remove from baking sheet to a wire rack to cool. Spread half of the cookies with Vanilla Frosting. Top with remaining cookies. Top with a small amount of frosting and a pecan half.

Vanilla Frosting

¼ cup butter, softened
2½ cups sifted powdered sugar
1 egg white
½ teaspoon vanilla
Food coloring, optional

In a small bowl, cream butter. Add sugar alternately with egg white, beating until light and fluffy. Blend in vanilla. Tint with food coloring.

Citrus Slices

Makes about 7 dozen

1 cup butter *or* margarine, softened
½ cup granulated sugar
½ cup packed brown sugar
1 egg
1 teaspoon grated orange peel
1 teaspoon grated lemon peel
¼ cup orange juice
1 teaspoon vanilla
3 cups all-purpose flour
½ teaspoon salt
¼ teaspoon baking soda
½ cup ground pecans

In a large mixing bowl, cream butter and sugars until smooth. Add egg, fruit peels, juice, and vanilla; blend well. Stir together flour, salt, and baking soda. Gradually add dry ingredients to creamed mixture; blend well. Stir in pecans. Divide dough in half. Shape each half into a 6½-inch roll. Wrap in plastic wrap and chill overnight. Cut into ⅛-inch slices. Place 1 inch apart on an ungreased baking sheet. Bake at 375° F. for 12 minutes or until edges are lightly browned. Remove from baking sheet to a wire rack to cool.

Rolled and Refrigerated Cookies

Brown Sugar Icebox Cookies
Makes about 5 dozen

In a large mixing bowl, combine sugars, eggs, and shortening; cream until light and fluffy. Stir together flour, baking soda, salt, and cinnamon. Gradually add dry ingredients to creamed mixture; blend well. Stir in pecans. Divide dough into thirds. Wrap in plastic wrap and chill overnight. Cut dough into ⅛-inch slices. Place on a greased and floured baking sheet. Bake at 375° F. for 8 minutes. Watch carefully: these cookies burn easily. Remove from baking sheet to a wire rack to cool.

1 cup packed dark brown sugar
1 cup granulated sugar
3 eggs
1½ cups vegetable shortening
4½ cups all-purpose flour
2 teaspoons baking soda
¼ teaspoon salt
1 teaspoon ground cinnamon
1 cup chopped pecans

Pinwheels
Makes about 7 dozen

In a large mixing bowl, cream shortening and sugar until smooth. Blend in eggs and vanilla. Stir together flour, baking powder, and salt. Gradually add dry ingredients to creamed mixture; blend well. Divide dough in half. Blend chocolate into one half. Cover and chill both doughs until firm. Roll each dough into a 12 x 9-inch rectangle. Place chocolate dough on top of plain dough. Roll to about ¼ inch thick. Roll up from the long side. Wrap in plastic wrap and chill until firm. Cut into ⅛-inch slices. Place on an ungreased baking sheet. Bake at 400° F. for 8 to 10 minutes or until set. Remove from baking sheet to a wire rack to cool.

¾ cup vegetable shortening *or* **butter/shortening mixture**
1 cup sugar
2 eggs
1 teaspoon vanilla
2½ cups all-purpose flour
1 teaspoon baking powder
1 teaspoon salt
2 squares (1 ounce each) unsweetened baking chocolate, melted and cooled

Baking sheets should cool before re-use; dough placed on hot baking sheets will spread too much. Work with 3 or 4 baking sheets to avoid waiting for them to cool.

To roll out dough, use a pastry cloth and stockinet-covered rolling pin for best results.

Pinwheels, this page
Chocolate Cherry Stripes, 36

Chocolate Cherry Stripes

Makes about 10 dozen

In a large mixing bowl, cream butter and sugar until smooth. Add egg and vanilla; blend well. Stir together flour, baking powder, and salt. Gradually add dry ingredients to creamed mixture; blend well. Divide dough into thirds. Stir cherries into ⅓ of the dough. Blend melted and cooled chocolate into remaining dough. Shape cherry dough into a 9 x ¾-inch bar. Shape chocolate dough into a 9 x 1½-inch bar. Wrap each bar in plastic wrap and chill until firm. Cut chocolate dough lengthwise in half. Brush cut sides of chocolate dough with hot milk. Brush both sides of cherry dough with milk. Place cherry dough between chocolate portions; press together. Wrap in plastic wrap and chill until firm. Cut into ¼-inch slices. Place on an ungreased baking sheet. Bake at 350° F. for about 10 minutes or until set. Remove from baking sheet to a wire rack to cool.

1 cup butter, softened
1½ cups sugar
1 egg
2 teaspoons vanilla
2½ cups all-purpose flour
1½ teaspoons baking powder
¾ teaspoon salt
½ cup candied cherries, diced
⅓ cup chopped walnuts
1 square (1 ounce) unsweetened baking chocolate, melted and cooled
Hot milk

Almond Slices

Makes about 7 dozen

In a large mixing bowl, combine almonds, flour, sugar, and cinnamon. Add butter and eggs; blend well. Divide dough in half. Shape dough into 2 long blocks 3 inches wide. Wrap in plastic wrap and chill overnight. Cut dough into ⅛-inch slices. Place about 1 inch apart on a baking sheet. Bake at 375° F. for 10 minutes or until edges are lightly browned. Remove from baking sheet to a wire rack to cool.

1½ cups sliced unblanched almonds
2 cups all-purpose flour
1 cup sugar
1 teaspoon ground cinnamon
1 cup butter, softened
2 eggs

Meringues and Macaroons

New England Macaroons

Makes about 2 dozen

1 egg white
¼ teaspoon salt
1 cup sugar
1 cup regular *or* quick-cooking rolled oats
¼ cup grated coconut
½ teaspoon vanilla

In a large mixing bowl, combine egg white and salt; beat until foamy. Gradually add sugar, beating until stiff peaks form. Fold in rolled oats, coconut, and vanilla. Drop batter by teaspoonfuls onto a greased and floured baking sheet. Bake at 350° F. for 12 minutes or until golden brown. Remove from baking sheet to a wire rack to cool.

Chocolate Mint Chip Meringues

Makes about 5 dozen

3 egg whites
1 teaspoon vinegar
1 cup sugar
3 drops green food coloring, optional
1 package (12 ounces) mint-flavored chips

Line a large baking sheet with a double thickness of waxed paper; set aside. Preheat oven to 350° F. In a large mixing bowl, beat egg whites and vinegar until foamy. Add sugar, 1 tablespoon at a time, beating until stiff peaks form. Blend in food coloring. Fold in mint chips. Drop meringue by teaspoonfuls onto prepared baking sheet. Place baking sheet in oven. Turn off heat. Let meringues stand in oven overnight. Store in a cool dry place.

Hazelnut Macaroons

Makes about 7 dozen

8 egg whites
⅛ teaspoon cream of tartar
2½ cups sugar
½ teaspoon vanilla
1 pound ground hazelnuts

Line a large baking sheet with uncoated paper; set aside. In a large mixing bowl, beat egg whites and cream of tartar until foamy. Gradually add sugar, beating until stiff peaks form. Blend in vanilla. Fold in hazelnuts. Cover and chill 2 hours. Drop batter by teaspoonfuls onto prepared baking sheet. Bake at 300° F. for 1 hour or until golden brown. Remove from baking sheet to a wire rack to cool.

Almond Meringue Bars

Makes about 4 dozen

In a large mixing bowl, cream butter and almond paste until smooth. Blend in egg and ½ cup brown sugar. Gradually add flour; blend well. Pat dough into a 12 x 9-inch baking pan. Bake at 325° F. for 20 minutes. Remove from oven. Spread jam over baked crust. Beat egg whites until foamy. Gradually add remaining ¾ cup brown sugar, beating until stiff peaks form a meringue. Fold in coconut. Spread meringue over jam. Return pan to oven for 20 minutes. Cool in pan before cutting into bars.

1 cup butter, softened
½ cup almond paste
1 egg
1¼ cups packed light brown sugar, divided
2 cups all-purpose flour
¾ cup raspberry jam
3 egg whites
½ cup flaked coconut

Italian Macaroons

Makes about 2½ dozen

In a large mixing bowl, combine ground almonds, sugar, salt, and almond extract. Add egg whites; beat until stiff. Sprinkle flour over batter; fold in with a rubber spatula. Shape tablespoonfuls of dough into balls. Place on a greased and floured baking sheet. Flatten balls slightly with the back of a spoon. Press one almond into the center of each cookie. Bake at 325° F. for 20 minutes or until lightly browned. Remove from baking sheet to a wire rack to cool.

1½ cups ground blanched almonds
1½ cups sugar
¼ teaspoon salt
1 teaspoon almond extract
3 egg whites
2 tablespoons all-purpose flour
Blanched whole almonds

Chocolate-Tipped Macaroons

Makes about 3 dozen

Line an 11 x 7-inch baking pan with aluminum foil; set aside. In a large mixing bowl, beat egg whites until foamy. Gradually add sugar, beating until stiff peaks form. Fold in almonds, cinnamon, and nutmeg. Spread batter in prepared pan. Bake at 275° F. for 20 minutes or until lightly browned. Cool completely in pan. Invert pan; peel off foil. Cut macaroons into bars. In the top of a double boiler, melt chocolate over hot but not boiling water. Dip one end of each macaroon into melted chocolate. Place cookies on a wire rack until chocolate is firm.

4 egg whites
1 cup sugar
2 cups blanched almonds
¼ teaspoon cinnamon
⅛ teaspoon nutmeg
2 squares (1 ounce each) semisweet baking chocolate

Meringue cookies absorb moisture readily. To keep the cookies from becoming soggy, store them in an airtight container.

No-Bake Cookies

Black and White Bars

Makes about 4 dozen

In the top of a double boiler, combine butter, sugar, cocoa, and vanilla. Cook over hot but not boiling water, stirring constantly until smooth. Add egg; cook for 5 minutes, stirring constantly. Stir in cracker crumbs, coconut, and nuts. Press mixture into a 9-inch square baking pan; cool. Spread cooled crust with Butter Filling. Chill 15 minutes. Spread with Chocolate Frosting. Chill well before cutting into small bars.

½ cup butter *or* margarine
¼ cup sugar
6 tablespoons unsweetened cocoa
1 teaspoon vanilla
1 egg, lightly beaten
2 cups graham cracker crumbs
1 cup flaked coconut
½ cup chopped walnuts
   Butter Filling
   Chocolate Frosting

Butter Filling

In a small bowl, cream butter until light and fluffy. Blend in pudding and milk. Gradually add sugar, beating until smooth.

½ cup butter *or* margarine, softened
2 tablespoons prepared non-instant vanilla pudding
3 tablespoons milk
2 cups powdered sugar

Chocolate Frosting

In the top of a double boiler, melt chocolate and butter over hot but not boiling water, stirring constantly.

3 squares (1 ounce each) semisweet baking chocolate
1 tablespoon butter

Choco-Peanut Balls

Makes about 2½ dozen

1 package (12 ounces) peanut butter chips
½ cup margarine
2 cups puffy rice cereal
1½ cups powdered sugar
1 cup chopped pecans
1 package (12 ounces) milk chocolate chips
½ cup vegetable shortening

In a large saucepan, combine peanut butter chips and margarine. Cook over low heat, stirring constantly until smooth. Remove from heat. Stir in cereal, powdered sugar, and pecans. Shape dough into 1-inch balls. Chill for 1 hour. In a small saucepan, combine chocolate chips and shortening. Cook over low heat, stirring constantly until smooth. Dip balls into chocolate. Chill before serving.

Mocha Pecan Balls

Makes about 2½ dozen

1 box (7 ounces) vanilla wafers
2 cups powdered sugar
⅔ cup chopped pecans
2 tablespoons unsweetened cocoa
¼ cup whipping cream
¼ cup double-strength cold coffee
Powdered sugar

In a blender or food processor, process the vanilla wafers to fine crumbs. Add 2 cups powdered sugar, pecans, and cocoa; blend well. Stir in cream and coffee; blend well. Shape dough into 1-inch balls. Roll the balls in powdered sugar. Chill well before serving.

Chocolate Oatmeal Drops

Makes about 4 dozen

2 cups sugar
½ cup milk
¼ cup butter
3 tablespoons unsweetened cocoa
¼ teaspoon salt
1 teaspoon vanilla
½ cup peanut butter
3 cups quick-cooking rolled oats

In a large saucepan, combine sugar, milk, butter, and cocoa. Bring to a boil; boil 1 minute, stirring constantly. Stir in salt, vanilla, peanut butter, and rolled oats; blend well. Drop by teaspoonfuls onto waxed paper. Let stand until set.

Cookies from a Mix

Spice Cake Bars

Makes about 2½ dozen

1 package (18.5 ounces) spice
  cake mix
½ cup butter *or* margarine,
  melted
3 eggs, divided
1 cup canned pumpkin
½ cup sugar
½ teaspoon grated orange peel
½ teaspoon grated lemon peel
¼ cup chopped walnuts

Set aside ¾ cup of the cake mix. In a large mixing bowl, combine remaining cake mix, melted butter, and 1 egg; blend well. Firmly pat crumb mixture into a greased 13 x 9-inch baking pan. Bake at 350° F. for 15 minutes. Remove from oven; cool. In a large mixing bowl, combine reserved ¾ cup cake mix, pumpkin, sugar, remaining 2 eggs, citrus peel, and nuts; blend well. Spoon batter evenly over baked crust. Bake at 350° F. for 15 minutes or until center springs back when lightly touched. Cool in pan before cutting into bars.

Peanutty Oatmeal Cookies

Makes about 2½ dozen

1 package (18 ounces) oatmeal
  cookie mix
1 egg
1 tablespoon water
½ cup chunky peanut butter
½ cup golden raisins
½ teaspoon vanilla

In a large mixing bowl, combine cookie mix, egg, and water; blend well. Blend in peanut butter. Stir in raisins and vanilla. Drop batter by rounded teaspoonfuls onto an ungreased baking sheet. Bake at 375° F. for 10 minutes. Remove from baking sheet to a wire rack to cool.

Chocolate Walnut Bars

Makes about 1 dozen

1 package (18 ounces)
  chocolate cookie mix
1 egg, lightly beaten
2 tablespoons butter, softened
½ teaspoon baking powder
1 teaspoon vanilla
½ cup chopped walnuts

In a large mixing bowl, combine cookie mix, egg, butter, baking powder, and vanilla; blend well. Spread batter in a greased 9-inch square baking pan. Sprinkle with nuts. Bake at 350° F. for 20 minutes or until golden brown. Cool in pan before cutting into squares.

Cookies from a Mix

Quick Chip Cookies

Makes about 3 dozen

In a large mixing bowl, combine cookie mix, egg, and water; blend well. Stir in chocolate chips and nuts. Drop batter by teaspoonfuls onto an ungreased baking sheet. Bake at 375° F. for 10 minutes. Remove from baking sheet to a wire rack to cool.

1 package (18 ounces) sugar cookie mix
1 egg
1 tablespoon water
1 package (6 ounces) semisweet chocolate chips
½ cup chopped walnuts

Vanilla Pudding Cookies

Makes about 2 dozen

In a large mixing bowl, combine pudding and baking mixes. Cut in shortening with a pastry blender or two knives until mixture resembles coarse crumbs. Add egg and milk; blend well. Shape dough into small balls. Place on an ungreased baking sheet. Flatten balls with a fork. Bake at 375° F. for 10 to 12 minutes or until golden brown. Remove from baking sheet to a wire rack to cool.

1 package (3 ounces) regular vanilla pudding mix
1 cup buttermilk baking mix
¼ cup vegetable shortening
1 egg
2 tablespoons milk

Lemon Meringue Bars

Makes 16 bars

In a large mixing bowl, combine cake mix, egg, and oil; blend until crumbly. Pat mixture into an ungreased 13 x 9-inch baking pan. Bake at 350° F. for 15 minutes. Cool crust slightly. Spread pie filling over crust. Spread Meringue over pie filling. Sprinkle with nuts. Bake 15 minutes or until Meringue is golden brown. Cool in pan before cutting into bars.

1 box (18.5 ounces) lemon cake mix
1 egg
⅓ cup vegetable oil
1 can (21 ounces) lemon pie filling
Meringue
½ cup chopped nuts

Meringue

In a large mixing bowl, beat egg whites until foamy. Add vanilla and cream of tartar; beat until soft peaks form. Gradually add sugar, beating until stiff peaks form.

6 egg whites
1 teaspoon vanilla
½ teaspoon cream of tartar
¾ cup sugar

Apricot Sesame Thumbprints

Makes about 3 dozen

1 package (18 ounces) oatmeal cookie mix
1 egg
1 tablespoon water
Sesame seed
½ cup apricot preserves

In a large mixing bowl, combine cookie mix, egg, and water; blend well. Drop batter by teaspoonfuls onto an ungreased baking sheet. Press thumb into center of each cookie to make an indentation. Sprinkle with sesame seed. Bake at 375° F. for 10 minutes. Remove from oven. Fill centers with apricot preserves. Remove from baking sheet to a wire rack to cool.

Gingerbread Cookies

Makes about 8 dozen

1 package (14.5 ounces) gingerbread mix
⅓ cup water
Vanilla Icing

In a mixing bowl, combine gingerbread mix and water; blend well. Cover and chill 2 hours. Divide dough into quarters. Roll out each quarter on a lightly floured surface to ¼-inch thickness. Cut out with lightly floured cookie cutters. Place on a large greased baking sheet. Bake at 375° F. for 6 to 8 minutes or until set. Remove from baking sheet to a wire rack to cool. Frost with Vanilla Icing.

Vanilla Icing

2 egg whites
½ teaspoon cream of tartar
2 cups powdered sugar

In a small mixing bowl, combine egg whites and cream of tartar; beat until foamy. Gradually add powdered sugar, beating until stiff peaks form.

Rich Chocolate Cookies

Makes about 3 dozen

2 eggs, lightly beaten
¼ cup water
1 package (15.5 ounces) brownie mix
½ teaspoon baking soda
¾ cup all-purpose flour
1 teaspoon vanilla

In a large mixing bowl, blend eggs and water. Stir in brownie mix, baking soda, flour, and vanilla; blend well. Drop batter by teaspoonfuls onto a greased and floured baking sheet. Bake at 375° F. for 10 to 12 minutes or until edges are lightly browned. Remove from baking sheet to a wire rack to cool.

Brambles

Makes about 4 dozen

1 package (11 ounces)
   piecrust mix
1 cup golden raisins
1 tablespoon grated
   orange peel
½ cup ground pecans
3 tablespoons orange juice
1 cup sugar
1 egg, lightly beaten
1 tablespoon cream

Prepare piecrust according to package directions. Roll out dough on a lightly floured surface to ⅛-inch thickness. Cut out with a floured 3-inch cookie cutter. In a blender, food processor, or food grinder, grind together raisins, orange peel, and pecans. Stir in orange juice and sugar; blend well. Place 1 teaspoonful of fruit and nut mixture on one side of each dough round. Fold in half. Seal edges with a fork. Brush with egg, then with cream. Place on a greased baking sheet. Bake at 375° F. for 8 to 10 minutes or until golden brown. Remove from baking sheet to a wire rack to cool.

Cherry Nut Cookies

Makes about 4 dozen

1 package (18 ounces) cookie
   mix
1 egg
1 tablespoon water
¾ cup chopped maraschino
   cherries, drained
½ cup chopped walnuts

In a large mixing bowl, combine cookie mix, egg, and water; blend well. Stir in cherries and nuts. Drop batter by teaspoonfuls onto an ungreased baking sheet. Bake at 350° F. for 12 to 15 minutes or until light brown around the edges. Remove from baking sheet to a wire rack to cool.

Italian Horns

Makes 8 to 10 servings

1 package (11 ounces) piecrust
   mix
1 teaspoon grated orange peel
1 cup whipping cream
½ cup sugar
1 teaspoon vanilla

Prepare piecrust mix according to package directions, adding orange peel to dough. Gather dough into a ball, wrap, and chill 1 hour. Divide dough in half. Roll out each half on a lightly floured surface to a 12-inch square. Cut into 1½-inch strips. Wrap strips around horn molds,* overlapping slightly. Moisten ends of strips with water; pinch to seal. Place on a large baking sheet. Bake at 400° F. for 10 to 12 minutes or until golden. Cool slightly on baking sheet. Gently remove molds. In a mixing bowl, beat whipping cream until soft peaks form. Gradually add sugar, beating until stiff. Blend in vanilla. Fill cooled horns with whipped cream.

*Available at gourmet shops.

Fried Cookies

Bowknots

Makes about 2½ dozen

In a large mixing bowl, beat egg yolks until light-colored. Gradually add sugar, beating until smooth. Blend in butter. Fold in whipped cream and cardamom. Stir together flour and salt. Gradually fold flour mixture into egg yolk mixture to make a soft dough. Wrap in plastic wrap and chill 3 hours or until firm. Divide dough in half. Roll out each half on a lightly floured surface to ⅛-inch thickness. Cut into 3½-inch strips. Cut a small slit lengthwise in the center of each strip; pull one end through the slit. Fill a large skillet with 1 inch oil. Heat oil to 375° F. Fry 3 or 4 cookies at a time about 1 to 1½ minutes or until golden brown. Drain on paper towels. Sift powdered sugar over warm cookies.

6 egg yolks
¼ cup sugar
1 tablespoon butter *or* margarine, melted
⅓ cup whipping cream, whipped
1 teaspoon cardamom
2 cups sifted all-purpose flour
½ teaspoon salt
Vegetable oil
Powdered sugar

Krumkake

Makes about 5½ dozen

In a large mixing bowl, whip cream until soft peaks form. Add eggs; blend well. Stir in sugar, butter, and almond extract. Gradually add flour; blend well. Drop batter by teaspoonfuls onto a hot krumkake iron.* Bake on top of the stove, turning iron over once while baking. Remove krumkake from iron with a spatula. Roll hot cookie around a krumkake roller or a 1-inch wooden dowel. Cool and remove from roller.

*Available in gourmet cooking shops.

½ cup whipping cream
3 eggs, lightly beaten
1 cup sugar
½ cup butter, melted
1 teaspoon almond extract
1¼ cups all-purpose flour

Cool cookies according to directions, either in the pan or on a wire rack. Do not stack, pile, or overlap warm cookies. Be certain cookies are completely cool before storing.

Italian Pizzelles

Makes about 3 dozen

In a large mixing bowl, cream margarine and sugar until smooth. Add eggs, 1 at a time, beating well after each addition. Stir in anise extract. Stir together flour, baking powder, and salt. Gradually add flour mixture to creamed mixture; blend well. Shape dough into 1-inch balls. Bake in a hot pizzelle iron* for 1 minute. Turn iron over and bake about 1 minute or until golden brown. Remove cookies from iron to a wire rack to cool. Store in an airtight container.

*Available in gourmet cooking shops.

1½ cups margarine, softened
1½ cup sugar
6 eggs
2 teaspoons anise extract
5 cups all-purpose flour
4 teaspoons baking powder
½ teaspoon salt
1 cup finely chopped nuts, optional

Polish Cheese Cookies

Makes about 2½ dozen

Press cheese through a sieve. In a large mixing bowl, combine egg yolks and sugar; beat until thick, about 5 minutes. Add cheese and salt; blend well. Add flour, 1 tablespoon at a time, beating just until dough forms. Dough will be sticky. Pat out dough on a floured surface to ¾-inch thickness. Cut into 2 x 1-inch rectangles. Fill a large skillet half full with oil. Heat oil to 375° F. Fry about 6 cookies at a time for about 15 seconds, turning to brown on all sides. Drain on paper towels. Serve immediately with sour cream and sugar.

16 ounces farmer's *or* pot cheese
4 eggs, separated
3 tablespoons sugar
¼ teaspoon salt
¼ cup all-purpose flour
Vegetable oil
Dairy sour cream
Granulated sugar

Snowballs

Makes about 2 dozen

In a saucepan, combine water, salt, and butter; bring to a boil. Remove from heat. Stir in flour all at once; blend until smooth. Add eggs, 1 at a time, beating well after each addition. Stir in raisins, citron, and rum. Fill a large skillet half full with oil. Heat oil to 375° F. With a metal spoon dipped in hot oil, cut off pieces of batter; fry them until golden brown on both sides. Drain on paper towels. Sprinkle with powdered sugar.

½ cup cold water
¼ teaspoon salt
½ cup butter
¾ cup all-purpose flour
3 eggs
2 tablespoons raisins
2 tablespoons chopped candied citron
1 tablespoon rum
Vegetable oil
Powdered sugar

Foreign Favorites

Empanadas

Makes about 3 dozen

In a large mixing bowl, cream butter and cream cheese until smooth. Add flour; blend well. Gather into a ball. Wrap in plastic wrap and chill until firm. Roll out dough on a lightly floured surface to ¼-inch thickness. Cut out with a floured 3-inch round cookie cutter. Place a teaspoonful of preserves in the center of each round. Moisten edges of each cookie with water. Fold in half; press edges together to seal. Place filled cookies on ungreased baking sheet. Bake at 375° F. for 15 to 20 minutes. Combine sugar and cinnamon. Roll cookies in sugar mixture while warm. Cool on a wire rack.

½ cup butter, softened
1 package (3 ounces) cream cheese, softened
1 cup all-purpose flour
1 cup fruit preserves
½ cup sugar
1 teaspoon cinnamon

German Sand Tarts

Makes about 2½ dozen

In a large mixing bowl, cream butter and 1¼ cups sugar until smooth. Add egg; blend well. Gradually add flour; blend well. Cover and chill overnight. Divide dough into quarters. Roll out one quarter at a time on a lightly floured surface to ¼-inch thickness. Cut out with a floured 2-inch cookie cutter. Brush rounds with beaten egg white. Combine remaining ¼ cup sugar and cinnamon. Sprinkle sugar mixture over rounds. Place on an ungreased baking sheet. Press a pecan quarter into the center of each. Bake at 350° F. for 8 to 9 minutes or until golden brown. Remove from baking sheet to a wire rack to cool.

1 cup butter, softened
1½ cups sugar, divided
1 egg, lightly beaten
2 cups all-purpose flour
1 egg white, lightly beaten
1 teaspoon cinnamon
Pecan quarters

If you don't have time to mix and bake cookies all at one time, store the batter in the refrigerator. Cookie batter will keep refrigerated in a tightly covered container for up to one week.

Apricot Linzer Cookies, page 53

Italian Anise Cookies

Makes about 2½ dozen

In a large mixing bowl, combine flour, eggs, lemon peel, sugar, rum, and anise extract; blend well. Blend in baking powder. Stir in almonds. Shape dough into a 3-inch-wide roll. Cut roll crosswise in half. Place halves on a greased and floured baking sheet. Bake at 350° F. for 1 hour. When the halves have cooled, cut into 1-inch-thick slices. Place cookie slices on their sides on baking sheet. Return cookies to oven for 10 minutes to dry.

2 cups all-purpose flour
2 eggs
1 tablespoon grated lemon peel
1½ cups sugar
¼ cup rum
¼ cup anise extract
2 teaspoons baking powder
1 cup slivered almonds

German Pfeffernusse

Makes about 5 dozen

Stir together flour, salt, pepper, and spices. In a large bowl, beat eggs and sugar until light-colored. Stir in flour mixture, almonds, and candied citron. Roll out dough on a lightly floured surface to ½-inch thickness. Cut out with a floured 1-inch cookie cutter. Place on a lightly greased baking sheet. Bake at 350° F. for 12 to 15 minutes or until golden brown. Remove from baking sheet to a wire rack to cool. Store in an airtight container.

1⅔ cups all-purpose flour
⅛ teaspoon salt
⅛ teaspoon black pepper
1 teaspoon cinnamon
¼ teaspoon allspice
¼ teaspoon cloves
¼ teaspoon nutmeg
¼ teaspoon mace
2 eggs
1 cup sugar
½ cup blanched chopped almonds
¼ cup chopped candied citron

European Bread Cookies

Makes about 5 dozen

In a large mixing bowl, combine flour, baking powder, and salt. Add eggs and sugar; blend well. Blend in shortening, lemon juice, and almond extract. Stir in almonds and raisins. Spoon batter into two 3-inch-wide loaves on a greased and floured baking sheet. Bake at 350° F. for 25 minutes. Turn oven off. Cut loaves into ½-inch slices. Place cookie slices on their sides on baking sheet. Return to oven for 10 minutes to dry.

2½ cups all-purpose flour
1 teaspoon baking powder
½ teaspoon salt
4 eggs
1 cup sugar
1 cup vegetable shortening, melted
1 tablespoon lemon juice
1 teaspoon almond extract
1 cup chopped blanched almonds
½ cup raisins

Apricot Linzer Cookies

Makes about 1½ dozen

2 cups all-purpose flour
½ cup powdered sugar
¼ teaspoon baking soda
¼ cup ground almonds
¼ cup granulated sugar
½ cup butter, chilled and cut in 1-inch pieces
2 egg yolks, lightly beaten
½ teaspoon vanilla
¼ teaspoon cinnamon
1 egg, lightly beaten
½ cup apricot jam

In a large mixing bowl, combine flour, powdered sugar, and baking soda. Stir in almonds and granulated sugar. Cut in butter with a pastry blender or two knives until mixture resembles coarse crumbs. Add egg yolks, vanilla, and cinnamon; blend well. Gather dough into a ball. Turn out onto a lightly floured surface. Knead lightly; shape into a smooth ball. Roll out dough between two sheets of waxed paper to ¼-inch thickness. Cut out with a floured 2-inch round cookie cutter. With a thimble, cut holes in centers of half of the cookies. Brush all the cookies with beaten egg. Place on a large greased baking sheet. Bake at 350° F. for 18 minutes or until golden brown. Remove from baking sheet to a wire rack to cool. Spread jam on whole cookies. Top each with a cut-out cookie.

French Tiles

Makes about 2½ dozen

½ cup butter, softened
½ cup sugar
½ teaspoon vanilla
½ cup sifted all-purpose flour
¾ cup sliced blanched almonds

In a large mixing bowl, cream butter and sugar until smooth. Blend in vanilla. Add flour; blend well. Stir in almonds. Drop batter by teaspoonfuls about 3 inches apart onto a buttered baking sheet. Bake at 400° F. for 8 to 10 minutes or until edges are golden brown. Cool 2 minutes on baking sheet. While still warm, press each cookie around a rolling pin to form tiles. Cool completely on a wire rack.

French Madeleines

Makes about 4 dozen

4 eggs
⅔ cup sugar
⅛ teaspoon salt
1 tablespoon lemon juice
1 teaspoon grated lemon peel
1 cup sifted cake flour
½ cup butter, melted and cooled

In a large mixing bowl, beat eggs, sugar, and salt until light-colored. Blend in lemon juice and peel. Gently fold flour into egg mixture. Gently fold in butter, 2 tablespoons at at time. Fill madeleine pan* ⅔ full with batter. Bake at 350° F. for 12 to 15 minutes or until firm and cookies begin to shrink from the sides of pan. Press narrow ends of madeleines to release them from the mold. Place, patterned side up, on a wire rack to cool.

*Available at gourmet cooking shops.

Russian Mushroom Cookies

Makes about 4 dozen

In a large mixing bowl, cream butter and sugar until smooth. Add eggs, 1 at a time, beating well after each addition. Blend in honey and sour cream. Stir together flour, baking soda, and spices. Gradually add dry ingredients and fruit peel to creamed mixture; blend well. The dough will be stiff. Divide dough in half. Cover and chill overnight. Preheat oven to 350° F. Shape half of dough into 1-inch balls. Make an indentation in the center of each ball with a lightly floured handle of a wooden spoon to make "mushroom caps." Place cookies, round sides up, on a greased baking sheet. Bake for 10 to 15 minutes or until golden brown. Shape remaining dough into stems 1 to 1½ inches long. Bake on a greased baking sheet for 10 to 12 minutes. Remove from baking sheet to a wire rack to cool. Dip one end of each of the stems into Almond Icing; press stems into indentations in mushroom caps. Let stand until set. Frost the undersides of the caps. Let stand until set.

¼ cup butter, softened
½ cup sugar
2 eggs
1 cup honey, heated and cooled
¼ cup dairy sour cream
5 cups all-purpose flour
1½ teaspoons baking soda
1½ teaspoons cinnamon
½ teaspoon cloves
½ teaspoon ginger
½ teaspoon nutmeg
½ teaspoon allspice
½ teaspoon pumpkin pie spice
1 teaspoon grated lemon peel
1 teaspoon grated orange peel
Almond Icing

Almond Icing

In a small bowl, combine all ingredients; blend until smooth.

3 cups sifted powdered sugar
1 teaspoon almond extract
8 teaspoons hot water

Greek Kourabiedes

Makes about 4 dozen

In a large mixing bowl, combine butter, 1 tablespoon powdered sugar, egg yolk, vanilla, almond extract, salt, and flour. Stir with a wooden spoon until just moistened. Mix with hands until well blended. Knead in pecans. Shape pieces of dough into 3-inch rolls. Place on a greased baking sheet. Pull ends down to form crescents. Bake on center rack of oven at 350° F. for 18 to 20 minutes or until bottoms are lightly browned. Sprinkle generously with powdered sugar. Cool on the baking sheet. Handle carefully as these cookies are very fragile.

½ cup butter, softened
1 tablespoon powdered sugar
1 small egg yolk
½ teaspoon vanilla
¼ teaspoon almond extract
⅛ teaspoon salt
1 cup plus 2 tablespoons all-purpose flour
½ cup broken pecan pieces
Powdered sugar

Pine Nut Cookies

Makes about 4 dozen

In the top of a double boiler, combine sugar and eggs. Cook over hot but not boiling water, stirring constantly until mixture is warm. Remove from heat. Beat until foamy; cool. Gradually add flour and lemon peel; blend well. Drop batter by ½ teaspoonfuls about 1 inch apart onto a greased and floured baking sheet. Sprinkle with powdered sugar and pine nuts. Let cookies stand 10 minutes. Bake at 325° F. for 10 minutes. Remove from baking sheet to a wire rack to cool.

1½ cups sugar
3 eggs
2½ cups all-purpose flour
Grated peel of ½ lemon
6 tablespoons powdered sugar
6 tablespoons pine nuts

Chinese Almond Cookies

Makes about 2 dozen

In a large mixing bowl, cream butter, lard, sugar, and salt until smooth. Blend in ground almonds, milk, and almond extract. Gradually add flour; blend well. Cover and chill 2 hours. Shape dough into 24 balls. Place on an ungreased baking sheet. Flatten with the bottom of a lightly floured glass to ¼-inch thickness. Press an almond in the top of each cookie. Bake at 350° F. for 12 to 15 minutes or until golden brown. Remove from baking sheet to a wire rack to cool.

½ cup butter *or* margarine, softened
½ cup lard
1 cup sugar
¼ teaspoon salt
½ cup ground blanched almonds
1 tablespoon milk
½ teaspoon almond extract
1¾ cups all-purpose flour
24 whole unblanched almonds

Brown Sugar Drops

Makes 2 dozen

In a large saucepan, combine brown sugar, butter, and corn syrup. Cook over low heat, stirring constantly until butter melts. Remove from heat. Stir in flour, ginger, and salt just until all ingredients are moistened. Drop batter by rounded teaspoonfuls about 4 inches apart onto a greased and floured baking sheet. Bake at 375° F. for 5 minutes or until cookies are set. Cool slightly on the baking sheet. Remove to a wire rack to cool completely.

¼ cup packed light brown sugar
¼ cup butter, softened
¼ cup dark corn syrup
½ cup all-purpose flour
1 teaspoon ground ginger
⅛ teaspoon salt

Holiday Cookies

Gumdrop Cookies

Makes about 3 dozen

4 eggs
2½ cups packed brown sugar
2 tablespoons water
¼ teaspoon salt
1 teaspoon vanilla
2½ cups all-purpose flour
1 teaspoon cinnamon
1 teaspoon baking powder
1 cup spice gumdrops, cut in halves
½ cup chopped walnuts

In a large mixing bowl, beat eggs until light-colored. Add brown sugar, water, salt, and vanilla; blend well. Stir together flour, cinnamon, and baking powder. Gradually blend flour mixture into egg mixture. Stir in gumdrops and nuts. Drop batter by teaspoonfuls onto a greased and floured baking sheet. Bake at 350° F. for 30 minutes. Remove from baking sheet to a wire rack to cool.

Leckerli

Makes about 4½ dozen

½ cup sugar
½ cup honey
2 tablespoons orange juice
¼ cup chopped candied orange peel
¼ cup chopped candied lemon peel
2¼ cups all-purpose flour
¼ teaspoon salt
1 teaspoon baking soda
1½ teaspoons cloves
1½ teaspoons nutmeg
1 tablespoon cinnamon
1 cup sliced almonds
1 teaspoon grated lemon peel

In a small saucepan, combine sugar and honey. Cook over low heat, stirring constantly until sugar dissolves. Remove from heat and pour into a large mixing bowl. Stir in orange juice and candied orange and lemon peel. Stir together flour, salt, baking soda, and spices. Add 1½ cups of the dry ingredients to sugar mixture; blend well. Knead in remaining flour, almonds, and lemon peel. Roll out dough on a lightly floured surface to ½-inch thickness. Carefully transfer dough to a greased waxed paper-lined baking sheet. Bake at 325° F. for 25 minutes. Invert onto a wire rack; carefully peel off waxed paper. Turn cookie right side up; cool. Cut into diamond shapes. Store in an airtight container 1 week to develop flavor.

Stained Glass Cookies

Makes about 3 dozen

3 tablespoons margarine	In a large mixing bowl, cream margarine, brown sugar, and molasses until smooth. Blend in water. Stir together flour, baking soda, salt, and spices. Gradually add flour mixture to creamed mixture; blend well. Cover and chill 1 hour. Cut out paper stars, bells, or other Christmas motifs. Trace onto a sheet of aluminum foil. Roll pieces of dough into ropes about ¼-inch wide. Outline the designs with ropes of dough. Press ends lightly together. Separate candies by color. In a blender or food processor, coarsely crush candies. Fill in dough outlines with the candies. Bake at 350° F. for 4 to 5 minutes or until cookie is set and candy melts. Cool on baking sheet.

- 3 tablespoons margarine
- ½ cup packed dark brown sugar
- ¾ cup molasses
- ⅓ cup water
- 3 cups all-purpose flour
- 1 teaspoon baking soda
- ½ teaspoon salt
- ¼ teaspoon cinnamon
- ¼ teaspoon nutmeg
- ¼ teaspoon ginger
- 1 bag (5¾ ounces) sourball candies

Chocolate Lebkuchen with Orange Glaze

Makes about 4 dozen

- 1¼ cups sugar
- ¾ cup honey
- 2 tablespoons water
- 1 package (12 ounces) semisweet chocolate chips
- 1 cup chopped walnuts
- ¾ cup finely chopped mixed candied fruit
- 2 eggs, lightly beaten
- ¼ cup orange juice
- 2¾ cups all-purpose flour
- 2 teaspoons cinnamon
- ½ teaspoon cloves
- ½ teaspoon cardamom
- 1 teaspoon baking soda
- 1 teaspoon baking powder
- Orange Glaze

In a large saucepan, combine sugar, honey, and water. Cook over medium heat, stirring constantly until mixture comes to a boil. Remove from heat; cool. Stir in chocolate chips, walnuts, candied fruit, eggs, and orange juice. Stir together flour, spices, baking soda, and baking powder. Gradually add to chocolate mixture; blend well. Gather dough into a ball. Cover and refrigerate for 2 days. Spread dough into a greased and floured 15 x 10-inch baking pan. Bake at 325° F. for 40 minutes. Cool in pan. Pour warm Orange Glaze over lebkuchen, spreading quickly over top. Cut cookies into diamond shapes.

Orange Glaze

- 2 cups sifted powdered sugar
- ¼ cup orange juice

In the top of a double boiler, combine powdered sugar and orange juice. Cook over hot but not boiling water, stirring often, until smooth.

White Pepper Cookies

Makes about 4 dozen

In a large mixing bowl, cream butter and sugar until light and fluffy. Add corn syrup and cognac; blend well. Stir together flour, cinnamon, cloves, white pepper, and ginger. Gradually add flour mixture to creamed mixture; blend well. Blend in almonds and orange peel. Gather dough into a ball. Cover and chill overnight. Divide dough into quarters. Roll out each portion between two sheets of waxed paper to ¼-inch thickness. Cut out with floured cookie cutters. Place on a large baking sheet. Bake at 350° F. for about 8 minutes or until golden. Remove from baking sheet to a wire rack to cool. Brush with Powdered Sugar Glaze.

1½ cups butter
1 cup sugar
1 cup dark corn syrup
2 tablespoons cognac
6 cups all-purpose flour
2 teaspoons cinnamon
1 teaspoon cloves
¼ teaspoon white pepper
1 tablespoon ground ginger
1 cup ground blanched almonds
4 teaspoons grated orange peel
Powdered Sugar Glaze

Powdered Sugar Glaze

In a small mixing bowl, combine sugar and egg white; beat until glossy and smooth.

2 cups powdered sugar
1 egg white

Springerle

Makes about 4 dozen

In a large mixing bowl, beat eggs until light-colored. Add sugar; beat until light and fluffy. Blend in lemon peel and anise extract. Stir together flour, salt, and baking powder. Gradually add flour mixture to egg mixture; blend well. Turn dough out onto a lightly floured surface. Knead for 8 minutes. Divide dough in half. Roll out each half to a ¼-inch thickness. Roll or press cookie designs into dough with a floured springerle rolling pin or flat springerle cookie mold. Cut apart with a sharp knife. Place on a lightly greased baking sheet. Cover with waxed paper and set aside at room temperature for 24 hours. Bake at 250° F. for about 18 minutes. The cookies should be white on top and light brown on the bottom. Remove from baking sheet to a wire rack to cool. Store in an airtight container one week before serving.

4 eggs
2 cups sugar
Grated peel of 1 lemon
½ teaspoon anise extract
4 cups all-purpose flour
½ teaspoon salt
1 teaspoon baking powder

Halloween Half-Moon Cookies

Makes 16

1¼ cups sugar
1½ cups vegetable shortening
½ cup instant nonfat dry milk
1 teaspoon light corn syrup
3 eggs
1½ teaspoons vanilla
4¼ cups cake flour
1½ teaspoons baking powder
¼ teaspoon salt
⅔ cup water

In a large mixing bowl, cream sugar and shortening until smooth. Blend in nonfat dry milk and corn syrup. Add eggs, 1 at a time, beating well after each addition. Blend in vanilla. Stir together flour, baking powder, and salt. Add dry ingredients alternately with water to creamed mixture, beginning and ending with dry ingredients; blend well. Pour about ½ cup batter on a greased and floured baking sheet. Smooth batter into a 3½-inch round. Repeat with 5 more rounds. Bake at 350° F. for 18 minutes or until lightly browned. Remove from baking sheet to a wire rack to cool. Holding cookies over frosting bowl, working quickly while fondant is still warm, frost cookies with Fondant Icing; one side with chocolate, the other with vanilla.

Fondant Icing

¾ cup water
2 pounds powdered sugar
¼ cup light corn syrup
½ teaspoon vanilla
2 squares (1 ounce each) semisweet baking chocolate, melted

In a large saucepan, combine water, powdered sugar, corn syrup, and vanilla. Cook over medium heat stirring constantly, to 100° F. on a candy thermometer. To 1½ cups of the icing, blend in melted chocolate.

Sour Cream Wreath Cookies

Makes about 2½ dozen

1 cup butter
1 cup sugar
½ cup dairy sour cream
1 teaspoon vanilla
3 cups all-purpose flour
¼ teaspoon salt
Red decorating sugar

In a large mixing bowl, cream butter and sugar until smooth. Blend in sour cream and vanilla. Stir together flour and salt. Gradually add dry ingredients to creamed mixture; blend well. Divide dough into quarters. Wrap each quarter in plastic wrap; chill about 1 hour. Working with 1 quarter at a time, break off pieces of dough and roll into 3-inch ropes. Press ends together to form wreaths. Place on a greased and floured baking sheet. Sprinkle with sugar. Bake at 375° F. for 10 to 12 minutes or until set. Remove from baking sheet to a wire rack to cool.

Caramel Crisp Bites

Makes about 5 dozen

20 marshmallows
20 light caramels
2 tablespoons water
2 tablespoons butter
1 teaspoon vanilla
3 cups crispy rice cereal
½ cup chopped pecans

In a large saucepan, combine marshmallows, caramels, water, and butter. Cook over low heat, stirring constantly until smooth. Remove from heat. Stir in vanilla, cereal, and nuts; blend well. Firmly press mixture into a greased 9-inch square baking pan. Let stand until cool. Cut into 1-inch squares with a knife dipped in hot water. Store in airtight containers.

Christmas Poinsettias

Makes about 5 dozen

2 cups powdered sugar
1 cup butter *or* margarine
2 eggs
1 teaspoon vanilla
½ teaspoon rum extract
3 cups all-purpose flour
1 teaspoon salt
1 cup shredded coconut
1 cup butterscotch-flavored chips, divided
  Granulated sugar
½ cup candied red cherries, cut in wedges

In a large mixing bowl, cream sugar and butter until smooth. Blend in eggs, vanilla, and rum extract. Stir together flour and salt. Gradually add dry ingredients to creamed mixture; blend well. Stir in coconut and ¾ cup butterscotch chips. Chill dough until firm. Shape into 1-inch balls. Place on an ungreased baking sheet. Flatten balls with the bottom of a glass dipped in granulated sugar. Press a butterscotch chip in the center of each cookie. Arrange cherry wedges in a circle around chips. Bake at 375° F. for about 12 minutes. Remove from baking sheet to a wire rack to cool.

Chocolate Date Nut Balls

Makes about 3 dozen

½ cup butter
¾ cup sugar
2 packages (8 ounces each) pitted dates, chopped
1 egg, lightly beaten
1 teaspoon salt
2 tablespoons milk
1 teaspoon vanilla
¾ cup chopped nuts
2 cups crispy rice cereal
2 cups chocolate jimmies

In a saucepan, combine butter, sugar, and dates. Bring to a boil. Cook over medium heat, stirring constantly until thickened. Add egg, salt, and milk; boil 2 minutes. Remove from heat; cool. Blend in vanilla. Stir in nuts and cereal. Shape dough into 1-inch balls. Roll in chocolate jimmies.

Index